W9-DIN-180

To Audrute

From Tete ... Mylin!

OTHER HELEN EXLEY GIFTBOOKS INCLUDE:

Go Girl!
To someone special Wishing you Happiness
To a very special Friend

OTHER BOOKS IN THIS SERIES:

To my very special Mother
To my very special Daughter
To my very special Sister

This book has been created from the smaller *To a very special*® Friend book, which has sold over one and a half million copies and is still one of our strongest sellers.

This large-format edition contains a larger selection of quotes with new illustrations by Juliette Clarke.

ACKNOWLEDGEMENTS
The publishers are grateful for permission to reproduce copyright material. Whilst every reasonable effort has been made to trace copyright holders, the publishers would be pleased to hear from any not here acknowledged. NATALIA GINZBURG: Extract from THE LITTLE VIRTUES, Copyright © 1962 by Giulio Einaudi editore s.p.a. Translation copyright © 1985 by Dick Davis Reprint from THE LITTLE VIRTUES by Natalia Ginzburg Published by Seaver Books, New York. C.S. LEWIS: Extract from THE FOUR LOVES, published by HarperCollins Publishers Ltd, 2002.
Important copyright notice: Pam Brown, Judith C. Grant, Charlotte Gray © Helen Exley 2007.

To a very special® Friend was first published in Great Britain in 1991 by Helen Exley Giftbooks. First published in the USA in 1992 by Helen Exley Giftbooks LLC. This new edition first published in 2007. Copyright © Helen Exley 1991, 2007. The moral right of the author has been asserted.

12 11 10 9 8 7 6 5 4

ISBN 13: 978-1-84634-182-3

A copy of the CIP data is available from the British Library on request. All rights reserved.

No part of this publication may be reproduced or transmitted in any form or by any means, electronic or mechanical, including photocopy, recording or any information storage and retrieval system without permission in writing from the Publisher.

Illustrated by Juliette Clarke. Edited by Helen Exley. Printed in China.

Helen Exley Giftbooks, 16 Chalk Hill, Watford, Herts WD19 4BG, UK.

www.helenexleygiftbooks.com

Dedication by Helen: to Zodwa Nkosi, my special friend.

"*To a very special*"® is a registered trade mark of Helen Exley Giftbooks.

To *my very special* FRIEND

ILLUSTRATED BY JULIETTE CLARKE

A HELEN EXLEY GIFTBOOK

harmony

Friends do not live in harmony merely,
as some say, but in melody.

HENRY DAVID THOREAU (1817-1862)

First of all things, for friendship,
there must be that delightful, indefinable state
called feeling at ease with your companion,
the one man, the one woman
out of a multitude who interests you,
who meets your thoughts and tastes.

JULIA DUHRING

Being with you is like walking
on a very clear morning –
definitely the sensation of belonging there.

E.B. WHITE (1899-1985)

secure, safe,
feeling loved

Seeing a good friend
is like going home,
or like tasting Mother's cooking.
I feel secure,
and need not protect myself.
"Here," I say,
"it is safe, for I am loved."

ARNOLD R. BEISSER, B.1925

Friendship, a dear balm…
A smile among dark frowns:
A beloved light:
A solitude, a refuge, a delight.

PERCY BYSSHE SHELLEY (1792-1822)

We need someone to believe in us
– if we do well, we want
our work commended,
our faith corroborated.
The individual who thinks well of you,
who keeps his mind
on your good qualities,
and does not look for your flaws,
is your friend.
Who is my friend?
I'll tell you: the one who
recognizes good in me.

ELBERT HUBBARD (1865-1915)

a refuge

to understand
and to be understood

One of the most
beautiful qualities of true friendship
is to understand
and to be understood.

SENECA (4 B.C.-65 A.D.)

Miraculously, our most serious situations
seem to lighten when we tell them to a friend
and feel that she has heard us.
The magic happens when a friend is able
to put herself in our place and, knowing us as she does,
to help us come to a decision
without necessarily solving the problem for us.
Being heard is a clarifying potion –
not made by any cosmetics company –
that helps us to see things clearly.

CARMEN RENEE BERRY AND TAMARA TRAEDER,
FROM "GIRLFRIENDS"

There, beside me

Don't walk in front of me,

I may not follow.

Don't walk behind me,

I may not lead.

Walk beside me,

And just be my friend.

ALBERT CAMUS (1913-1960)

My friend. You never expect too much of me.

You are glad when I succeed,

but failure makes no difference to you.

You give me all the help you can –

but, more important, you are simply there.

WENDY JEAN SMITH, B.1952

The most I can do for my friend
is simply to be his friend.
I have no wealth to bestow on him.
If he knows that I am happy in loving him,
he will want no other reward.
Is not friendship divine in this?

HENRY DAVID THOREAU (1817-1862)

True friendship comes when silence
between two people is comfortable.

DAVE TYSON GENTRY

Silences make the real conversations
between friends.
Not the saying but the never needing to
say is what counts.

MARGARET LEE RUNBECK

There was nothing remote or mysterious here
– only something private. The only secret
was the ancient communication between two people.

EUDORA WELTY (1909-2001)

*no need
to speak*

I always felt that the great high privilege, relief and comfort of friendship was that one had to explain nothing.

KATHERINE MANSFIELD (1888-1923)

United...
so strong together

So closely interwoven have been our lives,

our purposes, and experiences that, separated,

we have a feeling of incompleteness –

united, such strength of self-assertion

that no ordinary obstacles, differences,

or dangers ever appear to us insurmountable.

ELIZABETH CADY STANTON (1815-1902)

Two people holding each other up
like flying buttresses.
Two people depending on each other
and babying each other and defending each other
against the world outside.

ERICA JONG, B.1942

Like the shade of a great tree
in the noonday heat is a friend.
Like the home port with your country's flag
flying after a long journey is a friend.
A friend is an impregnable citadel
of refuge in the strife of existence.

AUTHOR UNKNOWN

defending each other

...It is that my friends have made

the story of my life.

In a thousand ways they have turned

my limitations into beautiful privileges,

and enabled me to walk

serene and happy in the shadow

cast by my deprivation.

HELEN KELLER (1880-1968)

What is a friend? I will tell you.
It is a person with whom you dare
to be yourself.

FRANK CRANE

Friend derives from a word
meaning "free".
A friend is someone who allows us
the space and freedom to be.

DEBBIE ALICEN

freedom

A real friend never gets in your way.

Unless you happen to be on the way down.

AUTHOR UNKNOWN

What do we live for,

if it is not to make life less difficult

for each other?

GEORGE ELIOT [MARY ANN EVANS] (1819-1880)

Trouble shared is trouble halved.

DOROTHY SAYERS (1893-1957)

It didn't matter that some of those friends
who were there for us we had not seen often.
What mattered is that when we needed them,
the tie was there.
And they came to help in any way they could.

NINA TOTENBERG, B.1944

It's not so much our friends' help
that helps us as the confidence and
knowledge that they will help us.

EPICURUS (341-270 B.C.)

What I cannot love, I overlook.

Is that real friendship?

ANAIS NIN (1903-1977)

A true friend is like the refrain
of a beautiful song.

F. PATARCA

To like and dislike the same things,

that is indeed true friendship.

SALLUST (86-34 B.C.)

Nothing can come between true friends.

EURIPIDES (484-406 B.C.)

a true friend

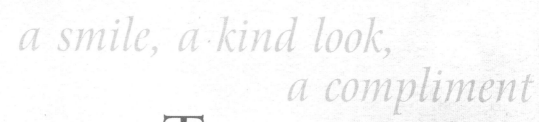

a smile, a kind look,
a compliment

The happiness of life
is made up of minute fractions –
the little soon-forgotten charities of a kiss,
a smile, a kind look,
a heartfelt compliment.

SAMUEL TAYLOR COLERIDGE (1772-1834)

Grief can take care of itself,
but to get the full value
out of joy you must have something
to divide it with.

MARK TWAIN (1835-1910)

Friends run across the road

with a plate of freshly-baked scones.

Friends fetch you to see the newly-born kittens.

Friends take cuttings for you.

Friends leave bags of apples on the doorstep.

Friends clear the snow off your side of the driveway.

Friends stop the milk when you forget.

Friends feed the cat.

Friends are absolutely indispensable.

Friends like you.

JUDITH C. GRANT, B.1960

...little things

Of all the things

which wisdom provides

to make life entirely happy,

much the greatest is the possession

of friendship.

EPICURUS (341-270 B.C.)

only friendship

Friendship is unnecessary,

like philosophy, like art....

It has no survival value;

rather it is one of those things

that gives value to survival.

C.S. LEWIS (1898-1963)

Friendship improves happiness,

and abates misery,

by doubling our joy, and dividing our grief.

JOSEPH ADDISON (1672-1719)

will do

The truth in friendship

is to me every bit as sacred

as eternal marriage.

KATHERINE MANSFIELD (1888-1923)

The moment we indulge our affections,

the earth is metamorphosed:

there is no winter, and no night: all tragedies,

all ennuis vanish – all duties even....

RALPH WALDO EMERSON (1803-1882)

when our world
threatens to dissolve

Our friendships are... the structures
that hold us in place
when our world threatens to dissolve.

ROSALYN CHISSICK, FROM "NEW WOMAN", AUGUST 1994

When the willow bends at the first hint
of troubled breezes, our friends
come running to see how they can help.
Sometimes friends know
when they are needed even before we realize it
ourselves, because we are accustomed to
letting them in on happenings of our lives.

LOIS WYSE

I never crossed your threshold
with a grief, but that I went without it.

THEODOSIA GARRISON (1874-1944)

When a friendship is born

We cannot tell the precise moment
when friendship is formed.
As in filling a vessel drop by drop,
there is at last a drop
which makes it run over,
so in a series of kindnesses
there is at last one
that makes the heart run over.

DR. SAMUEL JOHNSON (1709-1784),
QUOTED BY JAMES BOSWELL

Then little by little we discover

one friend, in the midst of the crowd of friends,

who is particularly happy

to be with us and to whom,

we realize, we have an infinite number

of things to say.

She is not the top of the class,

she is not particularly well thought of

by the others,

she does not wear showy clothes...

and when we are walking home

with her we realize that her shoes

are identical to ours

– strong and simple, not showy and flimsy

like those of our other friends....

NATALIA GINZBURG (1916-1991),
FROM "THE LITTLE VIRTUES"

...friendship, the ease of it,

it is not something to be taken lightly –

nor for granted.

Because, after breathing and eating

and sleeping,

friendships are essential

to our survival.

ADELAIDE BRY

Friends put the entire world
to rights over a cup of tea and a bun.

CHARLOTTE GRAY, B.1937

A friend, by a phone call,

a popping-in, a chance meeting,

a small unexpected surprise,

puts a little jam

on the day's bread and butter.

J.R.C.

"Stay" is a charming word

in a friend's vocabulary.

LOUISA MAY ALCOTT (1832-1888)

Friendship is a sheltering tree.

SAMUEL TAYLOR COLERIDGE (1772-1834)

It is the friends you can call up at 4 a.m. that matter.

MARLENE DIETRICH (1904-1992)

A friend is someone who arrives

when you have flu with a bag of oranges,

the thriller you wanted to read and a bunch of flowers.

They put the flowers in a vase,

make you a hot drink, do the washing-up – and go.

PAM BROWN, B.1928

when the rest of

Friends cherish each other's hopes.
They are kind to each other's dreams.

HENRY DAVID THOREAU (1817-1862)

When a friend asks there is no tomorrow.

GEORGE HERBERT (1593-1633)

A real friend is one who walks in
when the rest of the world walks out.

ALBAN GOODIER (1869-1939)

the world walks out

It is not that a person has occasion
often to fall back upon the kindness of friends;
perhaps we may never experience
the necessity of doing so;
but we are governed by our imaginations,
and they stand there as a solid
and impregnable bulwark
against all the evils of life.

SYDNEY SMITH (1771-1845)

Nothing makes the earth
seem so spacious
as to have friends at a distance;
they make the latitudes
and the longitudes.

HENRY DAVID THOREAU (1817-1862)

Life is nothing without friendship.

CICERO (106-43 B.C.)

The worst solitude is to be destitute
of sincere friendship.

FRANCIS BACON (1561-1626)

But every road is tough to me
That has no friend to cheer it.

ELIZABETH SHANE

without a friend

Friendship is based on chemistry and trust...

and why it happens or why

it rises and falls, and rises again,

is a mystery,

like a fine piece of music.

RICHARD LOUV, FROM "THE WEB OF LIFE"

It needs just a word in passing, a touch.

I think there is, in friendship,

an instant recognition – a kind of loving.

It needs just a word, in passing,

the touch of a hand.

H.M.E.

a kind

of loving

...who breaks the spell
of our loneliness

Happiness seems made to be shared.

JEAN RACINE (1639-1699)

Friends, companions, lovers,

are those who treat us in terms of our

unlimited worth to ourselves.

They are closest to us

who best understand what life

means to us, who feel for us

as we feel for ourselves,

who are bound to us in triumph

and disaster, who break the spell

of our loneliness.

HENRY ALONZO MYERS

A friend is a person with whom I may be sincere.

Before him I may think aloud.

I am arrived at last in the presence of a person

so real and equal, that I may drop even

those undermost garments of dissimulation,

courtesy, and second thought,

which men never put off,

and may deal with him with the simplicity

and wholeness with which one chemical atom

meets another.

RALPH WALDO EMERSON (1803-1882)

Just knowing I will

In loneliness, in sickness, in confusion –

the mere knowledge of friendship

makes it possible to endure,

even if the friend is powerless to help.

It is enough that they exist.

Friendship is not diminished by distance or time,

by imprisonment or war, by suffering or silence.

It is in these things that it roots most deeply.

It is from these things that it flowers.

PAM BROWN, B.1928

see you one day

Here at the frontier,
there are falling leaves.
Although my neighbours are all barbarians,

And you, you are a thousand miles away,
There are always two cups on my table.

AUTHOR UNKNOWN, TANG DYNASTY (618-906 A.D.)

...that is what being
a human being means

I love you not only for what you are,
but for what I am when I am with you.

I love you not only for what you have made of
yourself, but for what you are making of me.

I love you because you have done more than any
creed could have done to make me good, and more
than any fate could have done to make me happy.

You have done it without a touch,
without a word, without a sign.

You have done it by being yourself.
Perhaps that is what being a friend means after all.

ROY CROFT

Oh, the comfort – the inexpressible comfort

of feeling safe with a person – having neither

to weigh thoughts nor measure words,

but pouring them all right out,

just as they are chaff and grain together;

knowing that a faithful hand will take and sift them,

keep what is worth keeping,

and then with the breath of kindness blow the rest away.

DINAH MARIA MULOCK CRAIK (1826-1887),
FROM "A LIFE FOR A LIFE"

And all people live, not by reason of any care

they have for themselves,

but by the love for them that is in other people.

LEO TOLSTOY (1828-1910)

CHINESE OATH OF FRIENDSHIP, FIRST CENTURY

I want to be your friend

For ever and ever without break or decay.

When the hills are all flat

And the rivers are all dry,

When it lightens and thunders in winter,

When it rains and snows in summer,

When heaven and earth mingle –

Not till then will I part from you.

For ever